Selena

A biography by Sandhya Seshan, with Elvira Ortiz

SCHOLASTIC INC.
New York Toronto London Auckland Sydney
Mexico City New Delhi Hong Kong Buenos Aires

**Cover photograph by
© Al Rendon/Corbis**

4   5   6   7   8   9   10   23   12 11 10 09 08 07

Contents

Introduction

Selena was a great singer. She was on her way to the top.

People say that she could have been the greatest singer ever. They say that she could have had more fans than Janet Jackson, Gloria Estefan, and Madonna put together.

Maybe they're right. Selena had Spanish-speaking fans *and* English-speaking fans. She also had a lot of talent. And she worked very hard.

But Selena was killed when she was only 23. So we'll never know what could have happened.

This is Selena's story.

Selena had a nice family. And she was a happy kid.

1 A Star Is Born

Selena Quintanilla was born in Lake Jackson, Texas. The day was April 16, 1971.

Selena's family was Mexican-American. She had an older brother called A.B. She had an older sister named Suzette. And her parents' names were Marcella and Abraham. They were all very close.

As Selena grew up, she liked to do many things. She liked to play football, skate, and ride bikes with her friends.

She also had a special hobby she loved. She made clothes for her dolls. And when she got older, she made clothes for people.

She never stopped—even when she was a star.

Selena also liked school. She was a good student. One teacher said, "Selena was happy and friendly. She wanted to learn. And she wanted to do well. She was the kind of kid that you would like to have in class."

Even as a kid, Selena had fans!

What singer do you like best? Have you ever heard Selena's music?

Selena's dad taught his kids to play music. Soon, the family started a band.

2 Family Life

Si nos queremos todos,
el mundo va a cambiar.
If we love each other,
the world will change.
   "No Quiero Saber" ("I Don't Want to Know"), 1990

Selena's whole family loved music. When her dad was a teenager, he was in a band. It was called the Dinos. They worked really hard. But they never had any hit songs.

Selena's dad left the band. But he didn't stop playing music. Years later, he began to teach A.B. and Suzette to play music. A.B. played the guitar. And Suzette played the drums.

Selena felt left out. So she did something about it. "I got this old song book of my dad's. And I started singing in front of my family," Selena said.

Selena was a tiny girl. But she had a big, loud voice. "My dad saw that I learned those songs right away. And my timing was really good." So her father began to teach Selena, too.

In 1980, Selena was nine years old. That year, her dad opened a Mexican restaurant. It was called Papa Gayos. Selena's mom helped cook.

The family built a stage in the restaurant. Selena's dad had people come and play music. Sometimes Selena, A.B., and Suzette would sing and play with other bands.

A.B. played bass. Suzette played drums. And Selena would sing. Everyone who heard Selena liked her. She could sing really well.

Singing and playing music wasn't easy. It took a lot of hard work. The kids came home right after school each day. They played their songs over and over. Mr. Quintanilla made sure they worked hard.

Selena's dad wanted the kids to learn songs in Spanish. But Selena didn't know Spanish very well. So her dad would often sit with her and teach her some Spanish.

The family's restaurant was open for only one year. When Selena was ten, her parents had to close it. They didn't make enough money to pay the bills. The Quintanillas had to leave their home and stay with family.

Then they bought an old bus. They

started driving around, playing music.

They called their band Selena and Company. They played at little clubs, parties, and weddings.

The family added a guitar player and a keyboard player to the band. They also changed the band's name to *Selena y los Dinos*. That means "Selena and the Dinos." And young Selena **designed** the clothes for everyone in the band.

Those were hard times for the family. They didn't have much money. But they stayed close. They helped each other.

They also **believed** that Selena would be a star some day. She was such a good singer! "I always knew that Selena was going to make it. She had that special thing that makes an artist," her father said.

Selena and the Dinos started to play their own kind of music.

3 Her Own Style

Todos, las manos en alto
Y griten, griten con locura
Everyone, throw your hands in the air
And yell, yell like crazy
   "Baila Esta Cumbia" ("Dance the Cumbia"), 1990

Selena and the Dinos played **Tejano** music. The word *Tejano* means "Texan." The Mexican-Americans who live near the border between Texas and Mexico are called Tejano. The language they speak is also called Tejano. It is a blend of Spanish and English.

Tejano music has its own sound. It is a mix of many kinds of music. Part of it comes from Mexican **folk music**. And part of it comes from German **polka**. But it also has Cuban beats and country music sounds.

Lots of people in Texas like Tejano music. Many Spanish-language radio stations play it. The beat is good for dancing.

Selena had always liked Top 40 music. So she added pop and rock sounds to her Tejano songs. That made her songs special. People liked her sounds. And they liked the words she sang.

Selena **recorded** her first song when she was 12. Her first **album** was put out in 1984. It was called *Mis Primeras Grabaciones (My First **Recordings**)*.

At first, Selena did more than make

music. She also went to Oso Junior High in Molina, Texas. She made it to the eighth grade there. But it was hard to play music and go to school.

Her dad wanted her to work harder on her music. So he took her out of school. Her teachers weren't happy. But her dad felt it was the right thing to do.

Still, Selena wanted to learn. So she kept studying. She took classes by mail. And she got her GED when she was 17. That meant that she had the same skills as someone who finished high school.

Selena always told her fans, "Stay in school. Learn as much as you can."

Selena turned 15 in 1986. She recorded a song called *"Dame un Beso."* That means, "Give Me a Kiss." Her brother, A.B., wrote the song. It became Selena and the Dinos' first hit. Both Spanish and Spanish/English radio stations played it.

That year, Selena was on a magazine cover for the first time. The magazine was called the *Tejano* **Entertainer**. Radio stations started asking her to come and talk on the air, too.

Then Selena put out her first big album. It was called *Alpha*. People loved Selena's voice. Her songs were easy to get into. And they were fun. It looked like Selena might become a big star.

Selena and the Dinos were becoming one of the top bands in Texas.

4 Star of Texas

"And the winner is . . . Selena!" In 1987, those words were heard again and again.

Selena was only 16. But she was the star of the Tejano Music Awards. She was up for many awards. She won "Female **Vocalist** of the Year." And she won the "People's Choice Award."

Her song "Give Me a Kiss" was also up for two awards. One was "Single of the Year." The other was "Song of the Year." And her band was up for "Most **Promising** Band."

Soon Selena had fans all over the country. And she had fans in Mexico, too.

5 Making It Big

In 1989, Selena got a big break. She signed a deal with a big record company.

The next year, she put out a new album. It was called *Selena and the Dinos.*

At the 1990 Tejano Music Awards, Selena was once again the star. She won "Female Entertainer of the Year." And she won "Female Vocalist of the Year." But the winning didn't stop in 1990. Selena went on to win both awards every year for the rest of her life.

Selena became more and more popular. In 1991, she recorded *"Buenos Amigos"* ("Good Friends"). It was her first hit that played on radio stations outside Texas. Now she had Spanish-speaking fans all over America.

The next year, even more people became fans of Selena. She put out another album called *Entre a Mi Mundo (Enter My World)*. Two of the songs on it became big hits in Mexico. They were *"La Carcacha"* ("The Old Car") and *"Como la Flor"* ("Like a Flower").

In September of 1993, Selena sang for 70,000 people at a show in Nuevo Leon, Mexico. She was the first Tejano artist to do well in that country. People called her the "**Latina** Madonna."

How do you think Selena felt about having so many fans and hit songs?

Selena had been singing about love for years. But now she was living it.

6 Romance

In 1988, Selena met Chris Perez. They met through a friend. Chris played the guitar. In 1992, he joined Selena's band. After a while, she started to like him.

Selena once said about Chris, "We were friends first. I never thought I wanted to marry a **musician**."

Chris and Selena spent time together on the road. Soon Selena's dad saw that they liked each other. He told Selena to stay away from Chris.

"I was a very strict father," her dad said. "I thought Selena was too young to have a boyfriend. She was also becoming a big star. And I knew she could be even bigger. I didn't want anything to take time away from her music."

Selena's dad fired Chris from the band!

Everyone was shocked. And Selena was very upset. Four months went by. Then Selena's dad let Chris join the band again.

Selena and Chris were married in 1992 at City Hall in Nueces County, Texas. She was 21. He was 22.

Selena's family got to know Chris. And they started to like him. Selena and Chris moved into a house in La Molina, Texas. Her parents lived next door. And A.B.'s family lived on the same block.

Selena was very happy. Her family and friends loved her. And her songs were big hits.

Selena's biggest fan would become her biggest enemy.

7 A Fan Club

Selena became more and more popular. By 1991, she had her own fan club.

Here's how it started. That year, she met a woman named Yolanda Saldívar. Yolanda was much older than Selena. But they became good friends. Yolanda wanted to start a fan club for Selena. And Selena's dad said it was okay.

Yolanda was in charge of the club. It cost $20 to join. Yolanda sent letters and T-shirts to people in the club. She also planned parties and events. In less than four years, 5,000 fans joined the club.

Yolanda seemed to be a great friend.

Selena was "crossing over." But she wasn't forgetting her roots.

8 Crossing Over

*Haz mañana un día
digno de esperar.*
Make tomorrow a day
worth waiting for.
"No Quiero Saber" ("I Don't Want to Know"), 1990

In 1994, Selena was 23 years old. She had already done a lot. She was taking college classes by mail. She was working hard. And her records were big hits.

Selena was also a good person. She helped others. She didn't smoke or drink. And she didn't do drugs.

In November, she got another big break. Selena and the Dinos signed a new deal. They would make their first English-language record. It would be Selena's **"crossover"** album. English-speaking fans would join Selena's Spanish-speaking fans.

The head of the record company was happy to sign Selena. "Selena is a lot like Madonna," he said. "She will be a big pop star."

That year, Selena also got her first part in a movie. The movie was called *Don Juan DeMarco*. It starred Johnny Depp. One of Selena's songs was in the movie, too.

But that's not all. Selena also won her first Grammy that year. The award was for "Best Mexican-American **Performance**."

Selena had another dream come true in 1994. She opened her first clothing store. The store was in her hometown, Corpus

Christi, Texas. It was called Selena Etc. Selena designed all the clothes in the store. And she designed all the jewelry, too.

Eight months later, she opened another store in San Antonio, Texas. She hired Yolanda Salvidar to run the stores.

But there was one more thing Selena wanted to do. She wanted to learn Spanish. So she went to Monterey, Mexico. She worked on her Spanish there. And soon, she spoke it well.

She said, "If I ever have children, I want them to know Spanish. It only makes you a better person—or even smarter—to know two languages."

Why do you think Selena wanted to learn Spanish?

Selena was on her way to the top. But she would never get there.

9 The End

In 1995, Selena played in Houston's Astrodome. Over 60,000 people came to the show.

She was also working hard on her next album. It would be called *Dreaming of You.* She was going to sing songs in English and in Spanish.

Selena was a star. But she had one big problem. Yolanda Salvidar wasn't doing a good job. Suzette and A.B. talked to Selena about it. They said Yolanda might not be a real friend. They thought Yolanda might be stealing money from the fan club and the stores.

At first, Selena wouldn't listen. She was sure A.B. and Suzette were wrong. Why would Yolanda trick her? After all, Yolanda was her friend.

Selena wanted to talk to Yolanda. On March 31, 1995, they met at a hotel. Yolanda was mad that the family had said she was stealing. They had also told her to stay away from Selena. And they didn't want her to run the fan club anymore.

The talk did not go well. Selena turned to leave. And Yolanda pulled out a gun. She shot and killed Selena.

Later, Yolanda was sad about what she had done. But it was too late. Selena was dead.

Selena went after her dreams. And she helped others go after theirs.

10 After Selena

Tú, tú llegaste a mi corazón
con tu querer, con tu alma
You, you came to my heart
with your love, with your soul
    "Tú Robaste Mi Corazón" ("You Stole
My Heart"), 1994

Selena was dead. Selena's family couldn't believe it. Their hearts were broken.

Thousands of fans came to Selena's **funeral**. They came from far away. They told Selena's family how sorry they felt. They said good-bye to Selena.

Today, people still remember Selena. Many young people want to be like her. A student at her old school said, "People around here never become rich or famous. But Selena did. We all looked up to her."

Joanne, another student, once met Selena at her store. Joanne wanted to design clothes. Selena told her to go after her dream. "I never used to feel good about myself," Joanne said. "But now I think, *You can do it. Just try a little harder.*"

Mr. Padron is the principal at West Oso High. He said that some students hadn't cared much about school. But Selena changed that.

Her neighbor, Lupe Lopez, said, "You could **relate** to Selena. I feel a lot of pride in her."

The Quintanilla family wanted to **honor** Selena. So they came up with a special plan. They formed a group to help kids stay in school. In 1997, the group gave $33,000 to schools in Texas. "This is something Selena would have wanted," her dad said.

A movie has been made about Selena's life. "We made this film to keep her spirit and her dream alive," said the **director**.

Jennifer Lopez played Selena in the movie. "I don't think I'll ever have a part like this again," she said. "I got to play such a great person."

Many people loved Selena. A student at the **University** of Houston said, "She was such a great person. She meant so much to the **Latino** people. We'll never forget her."

Why did people love Selena so much? What did they learn from her?

SELENA IN PHOTOS

"She wasn't stuck up," one 16-year-old fan from Los Angeles said about Selena. "She was a singer for the people. Everybody loved her."

In 1994, Selena was a star of Tejano music. In April, she played at the Texas Live Music Festival in San Antonio, Texas, and the crowd loved her.

Selena had lots of fans. They were Spanish-speaking and English-speaking.

At the 1994 Tejano Music Awards, Selena won "Best Female Entertainer" and "Best Female Vocalist." She and her brother, A.B. *(left)*, also won an award for the album *Selena Live*.

Selena started making clothes when she was a girl. In 1994, she opened a store to sell her own line of clothing. The store was called Selena Etc.

© PAUL S. HOWELL/HOUSTON CHRONICLE/CORBIS SYGMA

© AL RENDON/CORBIS

Chris Perez played guitar in Selena's band. She had always said that she would never marry a musician. But she did. Selena and Chris married on April 2, 1992.

In 1995, Selena recorded *Dreaming of You*. The album sold 175,000 copies on the first day. It was the second-fastest-selling album ever by a female singer. And it was the first mostly Spanish-language record to start off at number one on the Billboard 200.

On March 31, 1995, Selena was killed. In this photo, fans in Victoria, Texas, remember her one year after her death.

ABRAHAM QUINTANILLA JR.

Selena's parents, Marcella and Abraham Quintanilla *(seated),* with her sister, Suzette, and her husband, Chris, in 1996.

©AL RENDON/CORBIS

On the Mexican Day of the Dead, people remember those who have died. These things were put together to remember Selena.

© AP/WIDE WORLD

Lynette Hernandez, age 8, joined a crowd of Selena's
fans in Victoria, Texas, on March 28, 1996. **37**

Glossary

album *(noun)* a group of songs recorded on a CD, tape, or record

believed *(verb)* felt sure about something (related word: believe)

crossover *(adjective)* something that's in a new group. Selena's first albums were in Spanish. Her crossover album was in English.

designed *(verb)* planned how something should look or be made *(related word: design)*

director *(noun)* the person who's in charge of making a movie

entertainer *(noun)* a person who puts on a show for others

folk music *(noun)* music that is shared by

a group of people and passed down over the years

funeral *(noun)* a special event for someone who has died

honor *(verb)* to remember someone in a special way

Latina *(noun)* a girl or woman whose family came from Latin America (Mexico, Central America, or South America)

Latino *(noun)* a boy or man whose family came from Latin America

musician *(noun)* a person who plays music

performance *(noun)* a show

polka *(noun)* a fast dance where couples move around the floor in circles

promising *(adjective)* someone who is likely to do well

recorded *(verb)* put music or other sounds on a CD, tape, or record

recordings *(noun)* songs that have been recorded

relate *(verb)* to feel like you know about or understand someone

Tejano *(noun)* a Mexican-American who lives near the border between Texas and Mexico. Also, the language that Tejano people speak.

university *(noun)* a school you go to after high school

vocalist *(noun)* a singer